MY GRANDFATHER'S LIFE

GRANDPA, I WANT TO KNOW EVERYTHING ABOUT YOU

GIVE TO YOUR GRANDFATHER TO FILL IN WITH HIS MEMORIES
AND RETURN TO YOU AS A KEEPSAKE

chartwell
books

GRANDFATHER, TELL ME YOUR STORY

Grandpa, you are my hero and my heart. You are an inspiration, an ally, and an amazing man. From the very first time I looked into your kind eyes and you scooped me up in one of your famous hugs, I knew I had found a best friend for life.

You have been rooting for me since day one, offering me support, encouragement, and unconditional love. You are quick to offer praise but always know when I need to hear the unvarnished truth. You've helped me celebrate my triumphs and heal from my tragedies, and there is no one whose advice I value or trust more.

I already feel like I know you so well. I can tell when your bright smile is concealing a worry and the instant your good-natured laugh turns mischievous. But, even so, I long to know more. I want to learn all I can about where you came from and how you grew up so that I can achieve a deeper understanding of how you became the wonderful individual you are today and the fabulous grandfather that I adore.

I want to know it all—the best, the worst, the ordinary, the sublime and everything else in between. I want to know all about the hopes and dreams you had as a child and how those transformed as you grew into an adult. I want to know your thoughts, your feelings, and your secrets. You know they will stay safe with me!

Please don't hold anything back when you answer these questions, be as honest and forthcoming as you can. I'm eager for as many details as you can remember—nothing is trivial, it's all important to me. You are important to me.

Grandfather, please, tell me your story.

CHAPTER I

EARLY CHILDHOOD & HERITAGE

The familiar scent of your mother's skin,

the soft texture of your father's shirt,

the swirl of colors outside your bedroom window.

"YOU HAVE TO DO YOUR OWN GROWING NO MATTER HOW TALL YOUR GRANDFATHER WAS." —Abraham Lincoln

When and where were you born? What time of day were you born?

_____
_____
_____
_____
_____
_____
_____
_____
_____
_____
_____
_____
_____
_____
_____
_____
_____
_____
_____
_____
_____
_____
_____
_____
_____
_____

"EXTERNALLY, THE JOLLITY OF AGED MEN HAS MUCH IN COMMON WITH THE MIRTH
OF CHILDREN." —Nathaniel Hawthorne

Tell me any stories you know about your birth. Were you born at home?
In a hospital?

What is your middle name? Who were you named after?

What were your parents' names and birthdays? Where did they grow up?

"A HAPPIER MAN YOU WILL NOT SEE THAN HE, WHENEVER HE CAN GET HIS GREAT GRANDCHILDREN ON HIS KNEE." —Charles Lamb

How old were your parents when you were born?

"WHAT IS PAST IS PROLOGUE." —William Shakespeare

Tell me about your mother. What was she like? Did she work? What were her hobbies?

Tell me about your father. What was he like? Did he work?
What were his hobbies?

How did your parents meet? How old were they when they got married?

How far back can you trace your lineage? Who were the first members of your family to settle down where you currently live?

"PICTURES AND SHAPES ARE BUT SECONDARY OBJECTS AND PLEASE OR DISPLEASE ONLY IN THE MEMORY." —Francis Bacon

Tell me about your maternal grandparents. What were their names and where did they grow up?

Tell me about your paternal grandparents. What were their names and where did they grow up?

Do you have any siblings? What are their names, ages, and birthdays? Tell me a little bit about each of them.

"THE FUTURE INFLUENCES THE PRESENT JUST AS MUCH AS THE PAST."
—Friedrich Nietzsche

Using all five senses, describe your earliest memory. Describe what you look like in your baby pictures. Are you smiling? Are you crying? Is someone holding you?

"IF WE EXAMINE OUR THOUGHTS, WE SHALL FIND THEM ALWAYS OCCUPIED WITH THE PAST AND THE FUTURE." —Blaise Pascal

Tell me any stories you know about what you were like as a baby.

Did anyone in your family speak a language other than English? Who and what language did they speak?

What are some family holiday traditions you remember?

"WHAT IS HISTORY? AN ECHO OF THE PAST IN THE FUTURE; A REFLEX FROM THE
FUTURE ON THE PAST." —Victor Hugo

Describe what you remember about bedtime when you were very young. Which family members do you resemble the most, both in appearance and personality?

_____

_____

_____

_____

_____

_____

_____

_____

_____

_____

_____

_____

_____

_____

_____

_____

_____

_____

_____

_____

_____

_____

_____

_____

_____

"WHAT THEN IS TIME? IF NO ONE ASKS ME, I KNOW WHAT IT IS. IF I WISH TO EXPLAIN IT TO HIM WHO ASKS, I DO NOT KNOW." —St. Augustine

Is anyone in the family a veteran? Tell me about their service.

Who was the wacky relative in your family and what are some fun stories about them?

"THE BEST PROPHET OF THE FUTURE IS THE PAST." —Lord Byron

CHAPTER II

CHILDHOOD

A fruit flavored popsicle on a hot summer's day,
the whoosh of bicycle tires over wet pavement,
the sharp sting of a skinned knee.

"THERE ARE FATHERS WHO DO NOT LOVE THEIR CHILDREN;
THERE IS NO GRANDFATHER WHO DOES NOT
ADORE HIS GRANDSON." —Victor Hugo

Tell me all of the nicknames you had growing up and who gave them to you.

Describe some toys you had as a child. Which was your favorite?

"THE HISTORY OF MY LIFE MUST BEGIN BY THE EARLIEST CIRCUMSTANCE WHICH MY MEMORY CAN EVOKE; IT WILL THEREFORE COMMENCE WHEN I HAD ATTAINED THE AGE OF EIGHT YEARS AND FOUR MONTHS." —Giacomo Casanova

What was your favorite food growing up? How often did you eat it?

"WHEN THE PAST NO LONGER ILLUMINATES THE FUTURE,
THE SPIRIT WALKS IN DARKNESS." —Alexis de Tocqueville

Who were some of your childhood friends?

Are you still in contact with any friends from childhood?

What was the neighborhood you grew up in like?

Using all five senses, tell me what you remember about your childhood home.

"LOVE IS A SYMBOL OF ETERNITY. IT WIPES OUT ALL SENSE OF TIME, DESTROYING ALL MEMORY OF A BEGINNING AND ALL FEAR OF AN END." —Madame de Staël

Did you have your own bedroom? If not, who did you share it with?
Describe it.

Did you have any pets growing up? Tell me about them.

What were some of your favorite things to do?

_____

_____

_____

_____

_____

_____

_____

_____

_____

_____

_____

_____

_____

_____

_____

_____

_____

_____

_____

_____

_____

_____

_____

_____

"KNOWLEDGE OF THE PAST AND OF THE PLACES OF THE EARTH IS THE ORNAMENT
AND FOOD OF THE MIND OF MAN." —Leonardo da Vinci

What games do you remember playing?

"LOOK BACK, AND SMILE AT PERILS PAST." —Walter Scott

What do you remember about elementary school? Did you like it?

What were some of the chores you were expected to do as a child? Did you receive an allowance?

If you had money of your own as a child, what was your favorite way to spend it?

"WHAT YOU ARE, YOU ARE BY ACCIDENT OF BIRTH; WHAT I AM, I AM BY MYSELF.
THERE ARE AND WILL BE A THOUSAND PRINCES; THERE IS ONLY ONE BEETHOVEN."
—Ludwig van Beethoven

43

What were some of your childhood hobbies?

What types of candy did you like the best?

Describe some of your Halloween costumes. Did you go Trick-or-Treating? What scared you?

Tell me about someone who had a positive influence on you when you were young, like a coach or a teacher.

_____

_____

_____

_____

_____

_____

_____

_____

_____

_____

_____

_____

_____

_____

_____

_____

_____

_____

_____

_____

_____

_____

_____

"THERE IS A TIME FOR MANY WORDS, AND THERE IS ALSO A TIME FOR SLEEP."
—Homer

What was your favorite thing to wear when you were little? Describe it for me.

Where did you put things that you wanted to hide from everyone else?
Where did you stash your treasures?

What are some activities you remember doing outdoors when you were little?

What was your favorite animal growing up and why?

Describe a typical family outing from when you were a child.

"LET PARENTS BEQUEATH TO THEIR CHILDREN NOT RICHES,
BUT THE SPIRIT OF REVERENCE." —Plato

Where did you go, what did you do and how did you get there?

Describe one of your favorite memories from your childhood.

When you were little, what did you dream of becoming?

_____
_____
_____
_____
_____
_____
_____
_____
_____
_____
_____
_____
_____
_____
_____
_____
_____
_____
_____
_____
_____
_____
_____
_____
_____
_____
_____
_____

"TIME, WHICH CHANGES PEOPLE, DOES NOT ALTER THE IMAGE WE HAVE RETAINED OF THEM." —Marcel Proust

CHAPTER III

TEENAGE YEARS

A secret whispered to you by your first crush,
the wide grin of your best friend, the comfort
of your favorite jeans.

"GOOD OLD GRANDSIRE…WE SHALL BE JOYFUL
OF THY COMPANY." —William Shakespeare

Tell me all about your high school. What was the mascot?

_____

_____

_____

_____

_____

_____

_____

_____

_____

_____

_____

_____

_____

_____

_____

_____

_____

_____

_____

_____

_____

_____

_____

_____

_____

_____

_____

_____

_____

_____

"WHO SO NEGLECTS LEARNING IN HIS YOUTH, LOSES THE PAST
AND IS DEAD FOR THE FUTURE." —Euripides

What were some of your favorite subjects and why?

Describe a typical weekday evening after school. What types of extracurricular activities did you participate in?

Using all five senses, describe one of your most vivid memories from high school.

What are some slang terms or phrases that were popular at the time and what do they mean?

_____

_____

_____

_____

_____

_____

_____

_____

_____

_____

_____

_____

_____

_____

_____

_____

_____

_____

_____

_____

_____

_____

_____

_____

"FOR ONE SWALLOW DOES NOT MAKE A SUMMER, NOR DOES ONE DAY;
AND SO TOO ONE DAY, OR A SHORT TIME, DOES NOT MAKE A MAN
BLESSED AND HAPPY." —Aristotle

What are some of the things you would do when you hung out with friends?

How would your parents describe you as a teen?

Tell me all about when you learned how to drive. Who taught you?

"A MAN OF GREAT MEMORY WITHOUT LEARNING HATH A ROCK AND A SPINDLE AND NO STAFF TO SPIN." —George Herbert

Describe one of the most fun memories you have from being a teenager.

_____

_____

_____

_____

_____

_____

_____

_____

_____

_____

_____

_____

_____

_____

_____

_____

_____

_____

_____

_____

_____

_____

_____

_____

_____

_____

_____

_____

_____

"WE ARE ALL INSTRUMENTS ENDOWED WITH FEELING AND MEMORY. OUR SENSES
ARE SO MANY STRINGS THAT ARE STRUCK BY SURROUNDING OBJECTS AND THAT
ALSO FREQUENTLY STRIKE THEMSELVES." —Denis Diderot

What were some of the difficult aspects of your life during these years?

Who was your high school sweetheart? Where would you go on dates?

What would you wear when you were trying to dress up and look nice?

Describe five things that you had in your bedroom as a teen.

"THINK ONLY OF THE PAST AS ITS REMEMBRANCE GIVES YOU PLEASURE."
—Jane Austen

What are some of your favorite books or comic books you read as a teenager?

Describe your first job. How much did you make?

What responsibilities did you have around the house when you were a teen?

"AN EDUCATION ISN'T HOW MUCH YOU HAVE COMMITTED TO MEMORY, OR EVEN HOW MUCH YOU KNOW. IT'S BEING ABLE TO DIFFERENTIATE BETWEEN WHAT YOU KNOW AND WHAT YOU DON'T." —Anatole France

Describe the kind of clothes you wore on a typical day. Did you have a favorite piece of clothing?

"I WRITE SLOWLY. THIS IS CHIEFLY BECAUSE I AM NEVER SATISFIED UNTIL I HAVE SAID AS MUCH AS POSSIBLE IN A FEW WORDS, AND WRITING BRIEFLY TAKES FAR MORE TIME THAN WRITING AT LENGTH." —Carl Friedrich Gauss

Describe your hairstyle when you were in high school. What types of hairstyles were popular at the time?

What are three TV commercials you remember seeing a lot when you were a teen? Write down the jingles if you remember them.

What were some of your favorite movies? How much did it cost to see a movie in the theater?

Who were your favorite movie stars?

"GLANCE INTO THE WORLD JUST AS THOUGH TIME WERE GONE; AND EVERYTHING CROOKED WILL BECOME STRAIGHT TO YOU."
—Friedrich Nietzsche

What type of music was popular at the time? List some of your favorite songs and bands.

What were your aspirations when you were in high school?
How did you imagine your future?

Describe the most embarrassing thing that happened to you as a teen.

"IT IS MY FEELING THAT TIME RIPENS ALL THINGS; WITH TIME ALL THINGS ARE
REVEALED; TIME IS THE FATHER OF TRUTH." —Francois Rabelais

Tell me about three meals you would have for dinner.

_____

_____

_____

_____

_____

_____

_____

_____

_____

_____

_____

_____

_____

_____

_____

_____

_____

_____

_____

_____

_____

_____

_____

_____

_____

_____

_____

_____

_____

"THE MIND OF A HUMAN BEING IS FORMED ONLY OF COMPARISONS MADE
IN ORDER TO EXAMINE ANALOGIES, AND THEREFORE CANNOT PRECEDE THE
EXISTENCE OF MEMORY." —Giacomo Casanova

What were some of the newsworthy things going on in the world when you were a teenager?

Tell me about someone who had a positive influence on you.

If you had made a time capsule as a teenager, what are six things you would have put in it and why?

"TIME SOMETIMES FLIES LIKE A BIRD, SOMETIMES CRAWLS LIKE A SNAIL;
BUT A MAN IS HAPPIEST WHEN HE DOES NOT EVEN NOTICE
WHETHER IT PASSES SWIFTLY OR SLOWLY." —Ivan Turgenev

What was you most prized possession and why?

"LIFE IS SHORT AND WE HAVE NEVER TOO MUCH TIME FOR GLADDENING THE HEARTS OF THOSE WHO ARE TRAVELLING THE DARK JOURNEY WITH US. OH BE SWIFT TO LOVE, MAKE HASTE TO BE KIND." —Henri-Frédéric Amiel

What felt important to you during this time of your life? What were you passionate about?

Describe a memorable adventure you had with friends.

Tell me about a time when you broke the rules.

"JUST AS TREASURES ARE UNCOVERED FROM THE EARTH, SO VIRTUE APPEARS FROM GOOD DEEDS, AND WISDOM APPEARS FROM A PURE AND PEACEFUL MIND. TO WALK SAFELY THROUGH THE MAZE OF HUMAN LIFE, ONE NEEDS THE LIGHT OF WISDOM AND THE GUIDANCE OF VIRTUE." —Buddha

Tell me about a time when you went out of your way to help someone else.

_____

_____

_____

_____

_____

_____

_____

_____

_____

_____

_____

_____

_____

_____

_____

_____

_____

_____

_____

_____

_____

_____

_____

_____

_____

_____

_____

_____

_____

"KNOW THE TRUE VALUE OF TIME; SNATCH, SEIZE, AND ENJOY EVERY MOMENT
OF IT. NO IDLENESS, NO LAZINESS, NO PROCRASTINATION: NEVER PUT OFF TILL
TOMORROW WHAT YOU CAN DO TODAY."
—Philip Stanhope, 4th Earl of Chesterfield

What types of things did you enjoy doing when you weren't occupied with school or other responsibilities?

What was something at which you excelled?

Describe a situation when you utilized your superpower.

"OUR DEEDS DETERMINE US, AS MUCH AS WE DETERMINE OUR DEEDS."
—George Eliot

Tell me about a time you remember laughing uncontrollably.
What was so funny?

_____

_____

_____

_____

_____

_____

_____

_____

_____

_____

_____

_____

_____

_____

_____

_____

_____

_____

_____

_____

_____

_____

_____

_____

_____

_____

"AS I APPROVE OF A YOUTH THAT HAS SOMETHING OF THE OLD MAN IN HIM,
SO I AM NO LESS PLEASED WITH AN OLD MAN THAT HAS SOMETHING
OF THE YOUTH. HE THAT FOLLOWS THIS RULE MAY BE OLD IN BODY,
BUT CAN NEVER BE SO IN MIND." —Cicero

What were some cartoons or comics that were popular?
Which was your favorite?

Describe five things that were commonplace when you were a teenager that are obsolete now.

What do you miss the most about being a teenager?

"YOUNG MEN, HEAR AN OLD MAN TO WHOM OLD MEN HEARKENED WHEN HE
WAS YOUNG." —Augustus

CHAPTER IV

YOUNG ADULTHOOD

The laughter of friends after a good joke, a satisfying lunch at a roadside café, the pastel splendor of the sky when you come home at dawn.

"THE GOLDEN MOMENTS IN THE STREAM OF LIFE RUSH PAST US, AND WE SEE NOTHING BUT SAND; THE ANGELS COME TO VISIT US, AND WE ONLY KNOW THEM WHEN THEY ARE GONE." —George Eliot

When did you first move out of your parents' home? Where did you go?

What was it like to be on your own for the first time?

"DO THOU LOVE LIFE? THEN DO NOT SQUANDER TIME, FOR THAT IS THE STUFF LIFE IS MADE OF." —Benjamin Franklin

Did you go to college? If so, where? If not, why?

"THERE IS ANOTHER OLD POET WHOSE NAME I DO NOT NOW REMEMBER WHO
SAID, 'TRUTH IS THE DAUGHTER OF TIME.'" —Abraham Lincoln

Did you serve in the military? If so, where and what was it like?

What was the first job you had as an adult? What are some of the other jobs you had, and which one did you enjoy the most?

Did a particular person inspire you in pursuing a job or career?

"WE ONLY LABOR TO STUFF THE MEMORY, AND LEAVE THE CONSCIENCE AND THE
UNDERSTANDING UNFURNISHED AND VOID." —Michel de Montaigne

Where was your first apartment or home? Describe it. Did you live alone or have roommates?

_____

_____

_____

_____

_____

_____

_____

_____

_____

_____

_____

_____

_____

_____

_____

_____

_____

_____

_____

_____

_____

_____

_____

_____

_____

"THE HAPPINESS OF YOUR LIFE DEPENDS UPON THE QUALITY OF YOUR THOUGHTS: THEREFORE, GUARD ACCORDINGLY, AND TAKE CARE THAT YOU ENTERTAIN NO NOTIONS UNSUITABLE TO VIRTUE AND REASONABLE NATURE."
—Marcus Aurelius

Who were your close friends when you were in your twenties?

What is the most exotic place you've ever travelled and when did you go there?

Tell me about a risk you took and describe the outcome.

"ONE'S PAST IS WHAT ONE IS. IT IS THE ONLY WAY BY WHICH PEOPLE
SHOULD BE JUDGED." —Oscar Wilde

What were some of your favorite places to hang out?

_____
_____
_____
_____
_____
_____
_____
_____
_____
_____
_____
_____
_____

What was your favorite cocktail?

_____
_____
_____
_____
_____
_____
_____
_____
_____
_____
_____
_____
_____

"HISTORY IS THE VERSION OF PAST EVENTS THAT PEOPLE HAVE DECIDED
TO AGREE UPON." —Napoleon Bonaparte

Describe a typical Friday night out with friends.

Did you enjoy watching sports? Which teams did you like? Who were your favorite athletes?

Have you ever been in a fistfight? If yes, who with and what caused it?

_____

_____

_____

_____

_____

_____

_____

_____

_____

_____

_____

_____

_____

_____

_____

_____

_____

_____

_____

_____

_____

_____

_____

_____

_____

"LIFE IS DIVIDED INTO THREE TERMS—THAT WHICH WAS, WHICH IS, AND WHICH WILL BE. LET US LEARN FROM THE PAST TO PROFIT BY THE PRESENT, AND FROM THE PRESENT, TO LIVE BETTER IN THE FUTURE." —William Wordsworth

What is the most difficult physical activity you've ever done?

"IT IS NEVER TOO LATE TO BE WHAT YOU MIGHT HAVE BEEN." —George Eliot

Have you ever ridden a horse? A skateboard? A surfboard? In a hot air balloon? If yes to any, please elaborate.

Describe something you built yourself from scratch.

Describe the wildest party you ever attended.

_____
_____
_____
_____
_____
_____
_____
_____
_____
_____
_____
_____
_____
_____
_____
_____
_____
_____
_____
_____
_____
_____
_____
_____
_____

"IF YOU WISH TO SUCCEED IN LIFE, MAKE PERSEVERANCE YOUR BOSOM FRIEND, EXPERIENCE YOUR WISE COUNSELOR, CAUTION YOUR ELDER BROTHER, AND HOPE YOUR GUARDIAN GENIUS." —Joseph Addison

How old were you when you first experienced the death of someone close to you? Who was it, and how did their passing change you?

"I LEFT THE WOODS FOR AS GOOD A REASON AS I WENT THERE. PERHAPS IT SEEMED TO ME THAT I HAD SEVERAL MORE LIVES TO LIVE AND COULD NOT SPARE ANY MORE TIME FOR THAT ONE." —Henry David Thoreau

Have you ever been in the hospital due to an accident or an illness?
What happened?

Using all five senses, describe a moment when you felt invincible.

Do you feel that any responsibilities during your early adulthood prevented you from pursuing your dreams?

"WASTE NO MORE TIME ARGUING ABOUT WHAT A GOOD MAN SHOULD BE.
BE ONE." —Marcus Aurelius

What were some shows you liked to watch on TV?

"SWEET IS THE MEMORY OF DISTANT FRIENDS! LIKE THE MELLOW RAYS OF THE
DEPARTING SUN, IT FALLS TENDERLY, YET SADLY, ON THE HEART."
—Washington Irving

What did you do on holidays? Did you visit your parents?

Did you date a lot in your twenties? Did you have a steady relationship?

If you could have visited one place in the years just after high school, where would it have been?

"YOU MUST BECOME AN OLD MAN IN GOOD TIME IF YOU WISH TO BE AN OLD MAN LONG." —Cicero

Did you have any pets when you first lived on your own? If so, what kind and what were their names?

_____

_____

_____

_____

_____

_____

_____

_____

_____

_____

_____

_____

_____

_____

_____

_____

_____

_____

_____

_____

_____

_____

_____

_____

_____

_____

_____

_____

_____

"HIDE NOTHING, FOR TIME, WHICH SEES ALL AND HEARS ALL, EXPOSES ALL."
—Sophocles

What historical events do you remember from this period in your life?

What historical figure impressed you the most during this time?

What are you most proud of having accomplished in your early adulthood?

"MAN IS THE ONLY CREATURE WE KNOW, THAT, WHEN THE TERM OF HIS NATURAL
LIFE IS ENDED, LEAVES THE MEMORY OF HIMSELF BEHIND HIM."
—William Godwin

Did you have a favorite car, truck, or motorcycle? If so, tell me about it.

"HE IS INDEBTED TO HIS MEMORY FOR HIS JESTS AND TO HIS IMAGINATION FOR HIS FACTS." —Richard Brinsley Sheridan

Tell me something that I will be surprised to hear about you in your twenties.

Name a few of the books that made the biggest impression on you as a young adult.

Did you ever receive any awards or prizes when you were in your twenties?

"THE SUPERIOR MAN ACQUAINTS HIMSELF WITH MANY SAYINGS OF
ANTIQUITY AND MANY DEEDS OF THE PAST, IN ORDER TO STRENGTHEN
HIS CHARACTER THEREBY." —John Milton

What did you worry the most about during your early adulthood?

"MEMORY IS A NET: ONE FINDS IT FULL OF FISH WHEN HE TAKES IT FROM THE
BROOK, BUT A DOZEN MILES OF WATER HAVE RUN THROUGH IT
WITHOUT STICKING." —Oliver Wendell Holmes, Sr.

Are you still in touch with any friends or co-workers from this time?
If so, who?

What new technology surprised you and changed your life the most?

Describe how you looked and dressed on a typical day when you were twenty-one years old.

"TIME IS WHAT WE WANT MOST, BUT USE WORST." —William Penn

When you were in your early twenties, where and what did you imagine yourself to be at age fifty?

"THERE ARE ONLY TWO LASTING BEQUESTS WE CAN HOPE TO GIVE OUR CHILDREN. ONE OF THESE IS ROOTS, THE OTHER, WINGS."
—Johann Wolfgang von Goethe

Do you remember what you did and how you felt on your thirtieth birthday?

CHAPTER V

ADULTHOOD

Your children singing holiday songs, the smell of a
steak sizzling on the grill, dancing with your spouse
in the kitchen late at night.

"I WILL NEVER BE AN OLD MAN. TO ME, OLD AGE IS ALWAYS
FIFTEEN YEARS OLDER THAN I AM." —Francis Bacon

Tell me the story of how you met your spouse.

When and how did you propose? How old were you?

Using all five senses, describe a memory from your wedding day.

Describe the moment when you first learned that you were going to be a father.

"THE TWO MOST POWERFUL WARRIORS ARE PATIENCE AND TIME." —Leo Tolstoy

What do you like to do to relax?

"THERE NEVER WAS A TRULY GREAT MAN THAT WAS NOT AT THE SAME TIME TRULY VIRTUOUS." —Benjamin Franklin

What is your favorite meal? Have you ever cooked it for yourself?

What other countries have you travelled to and when?

What was your favorite family vacation and why?

"YET MY GREAT-GRANDFATHER WAS BUT A WATERMAN, LOOKING ONE WAY, AND
ROWING ANOTHER." —John Bunyan

Tell me about a difficult decision you had to make and describe the outcome.

"SWEET IS THE MEMORY OF PAST TROUBLES." —Cicero

Who is someone you admire and why?

What is something that you consider to be a guilty pleasure and how often do you indulge in it?

What is a skill or talent you have that might surprise people?

"TIME IS A SORT OF RIVER OF PASSING EVENTS, AND STRONG IS ITS CURRENT; NO
SOONER IS A THING BROUGHT TO SIGHT THAN IT IS SWEPT BY AND ANOTHER
TAKES ITS PLACE, AND THIS TOO WILL BE SWEPT AWAY." —Marcus Aurelius

What would your friends say are your best qualities?

"MEMORY IN YOUTH IS ACTIVE AND EASILY IMPRESSIBLE; IN OLD AGE IT IS
COMPARATIVELY CALLOUS TO NEW IMPRESSIONS, BUT STILL RETAINS VIVIDLY THOSE
OF EARLIER YEARS." —Charlotte Bronte

What is the proudest moment of your career?

Describe a typical workday.

What was your first major purchase as an adult? Please tell me about it in detail.

"I AM THE FAMILY FACE; FLESH PERISHES, I LIVE ON." —Thomas Hardy

Tell me about a time when you felt truly afraid.

"WHY IS IT THAT OUR MEMORY IS GOOD ENOUGH TO RETAIN THE LEAST TRIVIALITY THAT HAPPENS TO US, AND YET NOT GOOD ENOUGH TO RECOLLECT HOW OFTEN WE HAVE TOLD IT TO THE SAME PERSON?." —François de La Rochefoucauld

Describe the perfect weekend.

What are the five best concerts you've attended?

Describe an experience you had that made you feel really angry.

"HE THAT RAISES A LARGE FAMILY DOES, INDEED, WHILE HE LIVES TO OBSERVE THEM, STAND A BROADER MARK FOR SORROW; BUT THEN HE STANDS A BROADER MARK FOR PLEASURE TOO." —Benjamin Franklin

What are the top three qualities you value in other people and why?

"BE HAPPY FOR THIS MOMENT. THIS MOMENT IS YOUR LIFE." —Omar Khayyam

What are five foods you hate and why?

What would your teenage self say about your adult self?

What is a goal you set for yourself and achieved? How did you achieve it?

_____

_____

_____

_____

_____

_____

_____

_____

_____

_____

_____

_____

_____

_____

_____

_____

_____

_____

_____

_____

_____

_____

_____

_____

"TIME, WHICH WEARS DOWN AND DIMINISHES ALL THINGS, AUGMENTS AND
INCREASES GOOD DEEDS, BECAUSE A GOOD TURN LIBERALLY OFFERED
TO A REASONABLE MAN GROWS CONTINUALLY THROUGH NOBLE
THOUGHT AND MEMORY." —Francois Rabelais

What motivates you?

"NO MAN IS RICH ENOUGH TO BUY BACK HIS PAST." —Oscar Wilde

What gets you out of bed in the mornings?

CHAPTER VI

WISDOM

An exquisite sunset punctuating a relaxing day, the lilt of birdsong at dawn, the pleasure of a simple meal made with fresh ingredients.

"I AM AN OLD MAN AND HAVE KNOWN A GREAT MANY TROUBLES, BUT MOST OF THEM NEVER HAPPENED."
—Mark Twain

Describe the best gift you ever received. Why was it the best?

What are three moments in your life when you felt the proudest?

"OLD AGE AND THE PASSAGE OF TIME TEACHES ALL THINGS." —Sophocles

What is your biggest regret?

"WHAT WE CALL WISDOM IS THE RESULT OF ALL THE WISDOM OF PAST AGES. OUR BEST INSTITUTIONS ARE LIKE YOUNG TREES GROWING UPON THE ROOTS OF THE OLD TRUNKS THAT HAVE CRUMBLED AWAY." —Henry Ward Beecher

What is your favorite season and why?

If you could change on thing about yourself, what would it be and why?

If you could change one thing about the world, what would it be and why?

"THERE ARE NO SECRETS THAT TIME DOES NOT REVEAL." —Jean Racine

What is your favorite season and why?

Tell me about a memory that always makes you smile.

If you could pick one year as the best in your life, which would it be?

What do you consider to be your greatest achievement so far and why?

"STUDY THE PAST, IF YOU WOULD DIVINE THE FUTURE." —Confucius

Describe how being a grandparent is different from being a parent.

"NO MAN WAS EVER WISE BY CHANCE." —Seneca

What are three things you learned from your grandfather?

What was a pivotal event in your life and how did it change you?

What is something that you wish would go back to the way it used to be and why?

"PERFECT LOVE SOMETIMES DOES NOT COME UNTIL
THE FIRST GRANDCHILD." —Welsh Proverb

What advice would you give to your fifteen-year-old self?

"A FAMILY WITH AN OLD PERSON HAS A LIVING
TREASURE OF GOLD." —Chinese Proverb

What is your favorite way to spend an afternoon by yourself?

Name five places you've never been that you would like to visit and why.

Tell me something you wish you had spent more time doing when you were younger and why.

What are four life lessons you've learned that you think are important.

Tell me about a time in your life when you felt let down by someone or something.

If you could choose any famous person, living or dead, to spend the day with who would you choose and what would you talk about?

What are three things you wish you knew how to do and why?

"TIME FLIES OVER US, BUT LEAVES ITS SHADOW BEHIND."
—Nathaniel Hawthorne

What do you want your legacy to be?

"LOVE MANY THINGS, FOR THEREIN LIES THE TRUE STRENGTH, AND WHOSOEVER LOVES MUCH PERFORMS MUCH, AND CAN ACCOMPLISH MUCH, AND WHAT IS DONE IN LOVE IS DONE WELL." —Vincent van Gogh

Tell me a secret that you've never told anyone else.

What advice would you give to your twenty-five-year-old self?

What do you do when you feel lonely?

"THE VALUE OF LIFE LIES NOT IN THE LENGTH OF DAYS, BUT IN THE USE WE MAKE
OF THEM.. WHETHER YOU FIND SATISFACTION IN LIFE DEPENDS NOT ON YOUR
TALE OF YEARS, BUT ON YOUR WILL." —Michel de Montaigne

If you could choose one day from your past to relive, which day would you pick and why?

"WE SHOULD NOT LOOK BACK UNLESS IT IS TO DERIVE USEFUL LESSONS FROM PAST ERRORS, AND FOR THE PURPOSE OF PROFITING BY DEARLY BOUGHT EXPERIENCE." —George Washington

What is something that seems like a blessing but really is a curse and why?

What are your spiritual beliefs?

If you could travel back in time to any moment in history, what would you choose and why?

_____

_____

_____

_____

_____

_____

_____

_____

_____

_____

_____

_____

_____

_____

_____

_____

_____

_____

_____

_____

_____

_____

_____

_____

_____

"KNOWLEDGE COMES, BUT WISDOM LINGERS." —Alfred Lord Tennyson

What would you say is life's purpose? Have you fulfilled it yet?

"THE YOUNG MAN KNOWS THE RULES, BUT THE OLD MAN KNOWS
THE EXCEPTIONS." —Oliver Wendell Holmes, Sr.

If you won a million dollars in the lottery, how would you spend the money?

If there was a movie made about your life, what would it be called and what actor would play you?

What animal is your spirit animal and why?

"LET ALL YOUR THINGS HAVE THEIR PLACES; LET EACH PART OF YOUR BUSINESS HAVE ITS TIME." —Benjamin Franklin

Inspiring | Educating | Creating | Entertaining

© 2021 by Quarto Publishing Group USA Inc.

This edition published in 2022 by Chartwell Books,
an imprint of The Quarto Group,
142 West 36th Street, 4th Floor,
New York, NY 10018, USA
T (212) 779-4972 f (212) 779-6058
www.QuartoKnows.com

Previously published in 2021 by Chartwell Books, an imprint of The Quarto Group,
142 West 36th Street, 4th Floor, New York, NY 10018, USA

Chartwell titles are also available at discount for retail, wholesale, promotional, and bulk purchase. For details, contact the special sales manager by email at specialsales@quarto.com or by mail at The Quarto Group, ATTN: Special Sales Manager, 100 Cummings Center, Suite 265D, Beverly, MA 01915, USA.

10 9 8 7 6 5 4 3 2 1

ISBN: 978-0-7858-4023-7

Publisher: Rage Kindelsperger
Creative Director: Laura Drew
Managing Editor: Cara Donaldson
Text: Christopher S. O'Brien
Cover Design: Beth Middleworth
Interior Design: Beth Middleworth

Printed in China